WOW!
CYCLING THE SILK
from Shanghai to London in thirty-six weeks

THE END

Go to the end of the book to start travelling East to West chronologically!

UNITED KINGDOM

POPULATION 66,650,000
CAPITAL CITY LONDON
LANGUAGE ENGLISH
CURRENCY BRITISH POUND £

SWITZERLAND

POPULATION 8,570,000
CAPITAL CITY BERN
LANGUAGE GERMAN, FRENCH, ITALIAN
CURRENCY SWISS FRANC

CROATIA

POPULATION 4,080,000
CAPITAL CITY ZAGREB
LANGUAGE CROATIAN
CURRENCY CROATIAN KUNA

MONTENEGRO

POPULATION 650,000
CAPITAL CITY PODGORICA
LANGUAGE MONTENEGRIN
CURRENCY EURO €

NORTH MACEDONIA

FRANCE

POPULATION 66,990,000
CAPITAL CITY PARIS
LANGUAGE FRENCH
CURRENCY EURO €

ITALY

POPULATION 60,360,000
CAPITAL CITY ROME
LANGUAGE ITALIAN
CURRENCY EURO €

ALBANIA

POPULATION 2,850,000
CAPITAL CITY TIRANA
LANGUAGE ALBANIAN
CURRENCY ALBANIAN LEK

GREECE

POPULATION 10,720,000
CAPITAL CITY ATHENS
LANGUAGE GREEK
CURRENCY EURO €

TURKEY

POPULATION 82,000,000
CAPITAL CITY ANKARA
LANGUAGE TURKISH
CURRENCY TURKISH LIRA

KAZAKHSTAN

UNITED KINGDOM
LONDON
PARIS
FRANCE
BERN
SWITZERLAND
ZAGREB
CROATIA
MONTENEGRO
PODGORICA
SKOPJE
NORTH MACEDONIA
ROME
ITALY
TIRANA
ALBANIA
GREECE
ATHENS
TURKEY
ANKARA
GEORGIA
TBILISI
BAKU
AZERBAIJAN

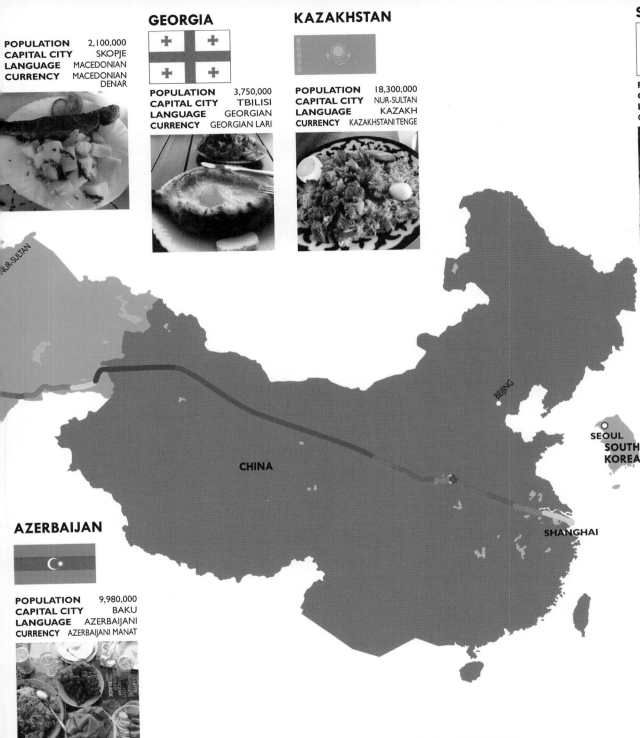

GEORGIA

POPULATION	2,100,000
CAPITAL CITY	SKOPJE
LANGUAGE	MACEDONIAN
CURRENCY	MACEDONIAN DENAR

POPULATION	3,750,000
CAPITAL CITY	TBILISI
LANGUAGE	GEORGIAN
CURRENCY	GEORGIAN LARI

KAZAKHSTAN

POPULATION	18,300,000
CAPITAL CITY	NUR-SULTAN
LANGUAGE	KAZAKH
CURRENCY	KAZAKHSTANI TENGE

SOUTH KOREA

POPULATION	51,700,000
CAPITAL CITY	SEOUL
LANGUAGE	KOREAN
CURRENCY	SOUTH KOREAN WON

NUR-SULTAN

BEIJING

SEOUL
SOUTH
KOREA

CHINA

AZERBAIJAN

SHANGHAI

PEOPLE'S REPUBLIC OF CHINA

POPULATION	9,980,000
CAPITAL CITY	BAKU
LANGUAGE	AZERBAIJANI
CURRENCY	AZERBAIJANI MANAT

POPULATION	1,400,000,000
CAPITAL CITY	BEIJING
LANGUAGE	CHINESE
CURRENCY	YUAN ¥

COUNTRY BY COUNTRY

CONCLUSION

LASTING MEMORY

Everything! I remember every day through diaries and spreadsheets, recording events and points of interest, impressions of landscapes, food, people and places, now captured in this great book. WOW!

TRIP *HIGHS*

- Christmas festivities in Cabris, France.
- New Year's Eve in Lake Como, near Milan.
- Three days at Promenois Castle in France.

TRIP *LOWS*

- Cycling along the treacherous cliffs in Croatia without a mobile phone and in the cold rain.
- Rejection from the locals in Dongcha, China, while searching for a place to stay the night.
- When Jianan and I depart ways in Turkey.

WORDS OF WISDOM

Start in spring and end in autumn, and think what you can give back to the locals.

WHAT TO DO DIFFERENTLY

- Undertake during warmer weather.
- Make the trip with someone like-minded.
- Perform warm-up and cool-down exercises before and after cycling.

ESSENTIAL EQUIPMENT

A phone and a strong bike lock. WOW!

ACHIEVEMENTS

I cycled 8567 km across 14 countries in thirty-six weeks, interviewed 10 startups in 10 countries, and held 10 seminars in 10 countries, sharing my spectacular story and inspiring others. WOW!

FAVOURITE COUNTRY OR PLACE

- France for always serving cheese, wine and dessert.
- Turkey for its breakfasts, *hamam, and* love of Koreans.
- Greece for its mythology, food, language and nature.
- Georgia for its food, wine and bathing. WOW!

LESSONS LEARNT

I am more confident, and proud for making my ambition come true, learning that I can correct mistakes, and emphasising the significance of the journey, not the destination. The map is now a series of highly personal experiences and lifelong memories, with an appreciation for the beauty of *giving and taking*. Exclude money, and people *give* each other love, care and support, and become friends. WOW!

South Korea feels more like an island than a peninsula. I long for Korea unification so that I can begin from Seoul next time!

FEELING WHEN FINISHED

A mixture of delight and disbelief, and trials and tribulations, but spurred on by superb hosts and newfound friends. It was a challenge but worth it. WOW!

WOULD I DO IT AGAIN?

Yes, but a different route. I am considering cycling from Berlin to Cape Town, South Africa. WOW!

RETURN TO SEOUL, SOUTH KOREA

I finish by cycling home 55 km from Incheon airport, deliberately arriving on the Korean New Year's Day.

Before making pancakes and serving *makgeolli* rice wine, my mum, dad, and cat greet me as if I have never left. I head for the local sauna and a well-deserved massage. It is great to be home. WOW!

LONDON   Awakening bright and early, I cannot believe that this is my last cycling day. WOW! My host accompanies me to the pub through stunning countryside. I am keen to learn from yesterday and start over.

I see London's red buses and tube stations, finally reaching the River Thames. On Westminster Bridge, I gaze at the Houses of Parliament and Big Ben, lit up in the night sky. WOW! Surrounded by people with umbrellas, I am a solitary bike in the rain. This contrast adds to the occasion and the enormity of my achievement. **I have arrived.** It has taken thirty-six weeks and been one very long journey, but it has been worth it. Definitely. WOW! Strangely, London may be my final stop, but it does not feel like the end of my trip. I must return home to Seoul for a conclusion, rather than finish as a tourist, visiting Tower Bridge and taking afternoon tea.

UNITED KINGDOM

NORTH SEA

LONDON

IFIELD

NEWHAVEN

ENGLISH CHANNEL

FRANCE

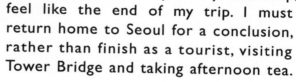

IFIELD

Dear Ain,

I am neither strong, brave, nor wise. I arrive in London tomorrow after failing to reach today's destination, starting too late and running out of daylight. The unlit roads are too dangerous at night, especially when cycling on the opposite side of the road! Annoyed for not rising earlier and taking the highway, I rest in a pub, ashamed that I cannot complete the last few kilometres, my mother ringing in my ear - *you should not think that the end is near, but think beyond that.* I was complacent and paid the price, my host picking me up in a van from the pub. I will return to the pub tomorrow and begin my final ride from there.

Paraphrased letter to a Korean friend written that day

NEWHAVEN

Disembarking the ferry late evening, Passport Control checks my identity, and questions my sanity for cycling mid-winter. WOW!

Looking for a hotel, I chat to a group who ask to ride my bike, to which I agree. Unfortunately, they attempt to perform tricks, falling backwards and shattering my backlight. They are apologetic and offer to pay for a replacement, but I blame myself, everyone handling my bicycle carefully until now. I am heartbroken. WOW!

ROUEN

My host shows me around by bike.

FRANCE

Dear Juhee,

When someone asks about my trip, I will recount the enormous amount of cycling, but also disclose how I had to cheat a little! Hats off to those who cycle the whole way. Sometimes I take a train, bus, ferry, or car to avoid danger. Perhaps the next person will do better. Blue comes from indigo! The map is no longer flat - my journey route, the good and not so good memories, and the people along the way, now play out in three dimensions. Artificial and virtual realities will never replicate or maximise these genuine experiences. I thank my home and Korea for enabling me to embark on this extraordinary tour.

Paraphrased letter to a Korean friend written that day

I study the many bullet holes at The Palais de Justice, badly damaged during heavy fighting in 1944, and visit Saint-Maclou Church, Rouen Cathedral, and The Big Clock.

My hosts gift me Calvados brandy, which I appreciate much later when I taste with my father. WOW!

I write this letter travelling to Rouen ...on a train to avoid the snow. WOW!

SEPTEUIL   I encounter a *Gilets Jaunes, Yellow Vests* demonstration with many police vans by the Palace of Versailles. There is mounting tension. I leave fast, marvelling at the palace on my right and the lake to my left.

France is the most hospitable country on my trip. I always have a local host during my twenty-four-day stay. My hosts in Septeuil cannot speak English very well, so we communicate with *Google Translate*. WOW!

Thank goodness for technology.

PARIS   **There is a cool bar where once a week, usually Thursday, one can perform poetry, a story, or a piece of music.**

I present my journey before standing once more to recite my favourite poem - *Ithaka*, by C. P. Cavafy, the inspiring poem I read aloud during my trip.

As I read into the microphone, I develop a lump in my throat, a feeling shared by other kindred travellers in the room.

Before leaving Paris, I cycle close to the Eiffel Tower as it reflects the golden sunrise. I am speechless. It is so beautiful. WOW!

MELUN

Contrary to my Sens letter, I enjoy cycling to Melun in the Paris suburbs, forty kilometres from the centre. I treat myself to a chocolate pastry on the way.

My hosts educate me on the different ethnicities in Paris, highlighting the successful cultural fusion with its resulting vibrant and diverse food and street scene. WOW!

SENS

Dear Juhee,

I need to cycle one more week, but it is just too hard. My legs feel like old rusty robot legs, and I have a bruised bottom. I want to finish so that I can rest and put everything down. Riding in winter is so painful despite the scenery. I do not want to see a bike for a while, fed up with pedalling hour after hour, caught up in counting kilometres and minutes, setting mini targets to motivate and combat boredom. I am exhausted, worn out and hungry. I need an all-over massage, and I am tired of talking to myself, desperately calling out for nonexistent company. I miss you. WOW!

Paraphrased letter to a Korean friend written that day

AUXERRE

Its scale is impressive from afar and my largest city after two weeks of cycling in France. It takes two and a half hours to look around, observing the soccer field and bicycle park before exploring the city centre with its cathedral overlooking the River Yonne.

I buy flowers for my host and her daughters.

Must-dos: The Cathédrale Saint-Étienne d'Auxerre with its magnificent gothic architecture. The Tour de l'Horloge XVth century clock tower with stunning gold dial and celestial hands.

ISLAND

My host drives me to Vezelay, a small town in Burgundy on top of a high hill, where the townsfolk are preparing for its annual end of January festival. There are flowers everywhere and a scarecrow decoration, together with carefully considered literature. I attend Mass at the gothic church and note how similar the priest's sermon is to those in Korea.

BLANCEY

Cycling cautiously through heavy snow and thick fog on snow-ridden icy roads, I arrive at this tiny village with its miniscule population of seventy-one.

My farmer host drives me to his hypnosis meeting in Dijon, but I struggle to understand the French conversations, questioning my attendance.

PROMENOIS Today is one of the hardest, cycling 45Km and 492m uphill in the freezing snow. I cry most of the way, my arms and torso covered in snow like the surrounding trees and fields, my tears turning to ice. WOW!

I race the final stretch, wiping the snow from my sunglasses, determined to reach my destination and catch a breath. On arrival, a man offers to show me to my host. I follow up more hills, despairing as I lose sight of the car. Despondent, I break down in tears, dragging my bicycle, unaware that my host is just around the corner.

CHEILLY-LÈS-MARANGES

I pass through Burgundy and Les Maranges villages, famous for the southern appellation of Côte de Beaune and its robust red wines.

My host takes me to an evening circus lesson. The next day, I go to a dancing *potluck party* in the Liernais town hall. Typically French and the initiative of a few villagers, it has grown over time as more bring musical instruments and refreshments. Everyone is dancing in rows to accordion music, skipping to the chorus and having a ball. WOW!

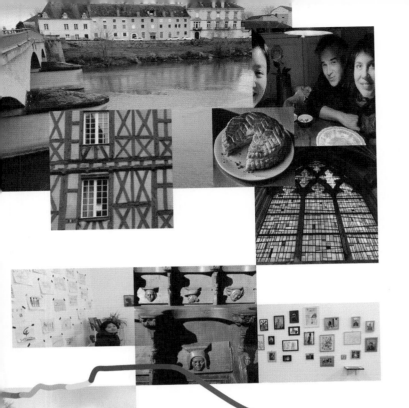

CHALON SUR SAÔNE

My hosts treat me to *Galette des Rois*, a traditional puff pastry filled with frangipane.

Walking through the city, I see how the old houses have a characteristic wooden cross construction, and discover occasional sculptural railings similar to those in Lyon. The stained church glass is a reflection of my impatient heart, chased by time. WOW!

BOURG-EN-BRESSE

Here start the flatlands. Hurrah! I visit the church and admire the wooden choir seat carvings depicting ordinary people with funny expressions.

NANTUA

Riding through the snow-covered foothills of the Jura Mountains uphill 700m to Nantua, I greet everyone with *Bonjour!* Cycling the alpine pass to the plains.

France is cold, but the people are warm.

GENEVA

I marvel at the pre-sunrise sky by Lake Geneva, surrounded by flying birds and stylish architecture, all creating something nostalgic and truly unprecedented. WOW!

LAKE COMO

I spend New Year's Eve at my friend's family house in Lake Como with eighteen people, enjoying good Italian food, drinks, games and fireworks. Never to forget!

New Year's Day is the day I turn thirty in Korean age. I am in the best scenery in Europe, with fantastic views of the lake and the snow-topped mountains. It is the best New Year's Day ever. WOW!

We return to Milan to buy a secondhand bicycle.

The owner retrieves the bicycle from her garage.

Instantly, I know that this bicycle is *my new horse,* handing over 180 Euros.

The kindness of strangers steers me back on track.

MILAN

Someone steals my bicycle in front of Luini bakery at five-thirty in the afternoon. WOW!

I am dumbfounded and think about giving up and returning to Korea. On reflection, I decide to purchase a secondhand bicycle, unhappy to quit in Milan after so many miles and so close to the London finish.

This misfortune coincides with my seminar at the hostel, initially with a single attendee. I post a map of my journey from Shanghai to London, asking if anyone would like to hear my story. Fifteen people arrive to make it especially memorable. WOW!

My host helps report my theft to the police to no avail. It is a shame not to finish with the same bicycle, especially after all we have been through together!

PIACENZA I cycle with my host to Cavalli Square. I love the Christmas projections on the buildings, especially those of the cherubims on the cathedral.

REGGIO EMILIA My host and I stroll in the eerie fog, entering the **Basilica di San Prospero** and viewing the lion statues in **Piazza San Prospero.**

(CABRIS)

I take a bus from Bologna to Genoa, then drive to Cabris in France, to spend Christmas with the friends and inspiration for my mammoth cycle ride. Even in their late fifties, they finished the trip in twenty weeks. WOW!

We stay in a 1970's house on the side of a mountain, surrounded by nature. Waking early, I spy the incredible red sky and pull up a chair to write my diary.

Cabris is the childhood home of the famous French writer, Saint Exupéry. The elementary school bears his name, and his *Little Prince* character is painted in restaurants and on street decorations. We pass by Saint Exupéry's house.

On Christmas Eve, we hike by moonlight through falling oak leaves to a hilltop village church, arriving for the *Provison* nativity play parade, where villagers of all ages participate in traditional Provence dress.

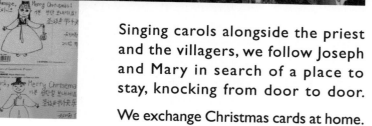

Singing carols alongside the priest and the villagers, we follow Joseph and Mary in search of a place to stay, knocking from door to door.

We exchange Christmas cards at home.

BOLOGNA   After dinner, I walk to Piazza Maggiore in the old town where a giant Christmas tree stands. I find the Basilica of San Petronio in the Palazzo Comunale, now the City Hall, and discover Neptune's Fountain. They look so mysterious under the moon.

The owner of Dolce Vita offers me a beer and a sandwich *on the house*. I make friends with everyone in the bar. WOW!

CESENA   I buy *Sanjoveje* wine, which means *Blood of Zeus*, for less than two euros per litre.

It is amazing how much wine Italy produces. Much is on tap.

I only want half a litre, but the assistant insists that I fill it up. So I do. WOW!

PESARO   **To avoid a harsh rainstorm, I ferry from Split to Ancona, then cycle north to Pesaro, where my host shows me around the town.**

There is a lovely opera house. Pesaro is the birthplace of musician Rossini, who wrote *Sevilla*'s *Barber,* and a master of comic opera, although his romantic tragedies are gaining recognition. I can discern Croatia across the Adriatic Sea.

SPLIT

I walk to the Boulevard near the port to witness the sunrise and again to admire the sunset.

In the afternoon, I take a long walk up Marjan Hill on the west side of Split, an oasis for those seeking natural stress relief and amazing panoramic views.

I also walk through the narrow, winding alleys in the Old Town, leading to Diocletian's Palace. I enjoy the Christmas decorations.

In light of cycling for two hundred days, I treat myself to Dalmation *pasticada* beef in sweet and sour sauce, served with fresh homemade gnocchi. Delicious. WOW!

MAKARSKA

I have a craving for bread, but everything in Croatia is shut out of season. There are no bakeries with usual stacks of bread in the window. Restaurant curtains are drawn. Empty apartments are *for rent* everywhere one looks.

Luckily, I find a petrol station with its integrated market, and select a chocolate snack and a chocolate bar.

While I sit in the cold and stare out to sea, I absorb every mouthful like a drought-ridden desert. WOW!

NEUM

I continue through Croatia until I encounter the Bosnia & Herzegovina coastal annexe.

I struggle with frozen hands at passport control, barely able to unzip my jacket. WOW!

Riding uphill then downhill, my thighs feel like sheets of ice, and the cold headwind is excruciating against my rain-soaked body.

Unable to control my freezing hands and aware that I can easily fall off the cliff if I lose my grip, I brake more than necessary.

My mother would call me *as stupid as a donkey* for riding in the winter rain. WOW!

Unfortunately, my phone is broken, and I cannot take photographs for a few days.

DUBROVNIK

Approaching a pedestrian crossing uphill, I see the much-wanted downhill. Changing gear, I cycle merrily downhill to encounter yet another incline, testing and pushing my patience beyond its limit when I reach the top again only to find it continues further uphill. WOW!

The oncoming traffic advances from on high and flashes its headlights but cannot stop to assist on such a busy road. Meanwhile, the forward-moving cars maintain full beam trying to avoid me, all adding to the drama. This section proves too hard and far too much, forcing me to cry uncontrollably and battle on through streaming tears. Then the traffic disappears, leaving only my headlight

and the crescent moon shining down from the west. Everything is pitch black with mountains on the right and the Adriatic Sea on the left, indiscernible to the night sky, except for the shadows cast by passing clouds. I pull myself together and continue uphill until finally, I complete the last hill and discover the bright lights of Dubrovnik in Croatia and its beautiful castle walls. WOW!

I stay for three days. Annoyingly, my phone is broken, so I am unable to take pictures. After my trip, I attempt to capture my harrowing experience in oils, determined not to be outdone by this lack of technology. WOW!

KOTOR

When I open my eyes, I face the breathtaking and overwhelming fiord. It feels like a misplaced tiny house in the nest of the great gods. WOW!

I visit the local Maritime Museum. Lace seems to be the most striking difference in attire between men and women. I learn that Montenegro's superb lace is revered all over Europe. I also learn about Captain Mako, who defeated the notorious Turkish Sultan, Ibrahim and his two hundred pirates, with only nineteen sailors and four cannons. Unfortunately, Captain Mako is forced to surrender when Ibrahim returns with three hundred pirates to attack the ship of Captain Mako's brother.

Folklore says that this naval skirmish results in the liberation of many Christians.

PODGORICA

I arrive in Podgorica, the capital city of Montenegro, and try to find the attractions, but as a newish city, it apears not to have many historical buildings. I leave the next day.

SHKODER

Six cyclists from various countries, including England, Germany, Norway, Sweden, Taiwan and Korea, stay at the Warm Shower house with our extremely warm and welcoming hosts.

After playing with the microphone the previous evening, I suggest Karaoke after dinner. Typically, everyone is awkward and embarrassed until I fetch my microphone and sing my favourite *Whale's Dream* song. Then everyone relaxes, and we sit on the sofa and sing a medley of carols together. It is great fun. WOW!

TIRANA

I learn that Albania is one of the oldest countries and that Albanians are strong and defiant. For example, Albanians accepted many Kosovo refugees when Serbia invaded, and hid countless Jews during the Nazi holocaust, including Albert Einstein, until he acquired a counterfeit Albanian passport.

Tirana is the capital city of Albania. I meet a dentist with a dental clinic who describes how low are the dental procedure costs and how the poor receive free medical care. Accordingly, customers travel from Italy and other countries.

Raki is the national drink of Turkey, popular in other Balkan conutries. Alcohol made from grape residue.

ELBASAN

I eat the distinctive *Bugache* bread and sip my cocoa-capped cappuccino in a local cafe while watching older men in fancy fedoras and black jackets, drinking coffee in tiny cups, conversing and reading newspapers. How better way to begin the day. WOW!

Before lunching at a taverna outside the castle gate, I take a pleasant walk along the ancient walls in the sunshine as the fedora-wearing older men cycle past.

Tomatoes, cucumbers, apples and tangerines are most common in the traditional market, alongside cheese and olives, even hair slippers, cots and carpets. Surprisingly, the fashion reminds me of the Korean *ajumma* middle-aged women.

OHRID

While Lake Ohrid is touristy, the town of Struga feels authentic and quiet. Famous poets plant the city park trees, and the River Drim runs clear where eel fishing was prevalent until recently. Installing an electric generator blocked the return path for eels to lay eggs before dying. Struga was known as *Enchalon* in ancient time, which means *eel*. There is *Man's Beach* in Struga next door to *Woman's Beach!*

- Breakfast at the Epinal Hotel in the city centre where the eggs, sausage, cucumber, tomato, red bean soup and bread are delicious. WOW!

- Walk down pedestrian Shirok Sokak Street, lined with romantic, colourful and neo-classical buildings.

- Visit the Old Bazaar with its pleasant small squares, water fountains and many cool Ottoman monuments.

- Sample Macedonian food and drink. Such as strong and yellow *Rakia* alcohol, *Tulshija* pickled vegetable salad, only eaten in winter, and bread covered in *Ajvar* paprika jam.

- See the amphitheatre of Heraklea Lynkestis, an ancient city founded by Macedonian King Phillip II in the middle of the 4th century BC. Heraklea is small, and its preservation is inferior compared with Ephesus in Turkey, but the pillars are noteworthy.

BITOLA

Bitola is the second-largest city in Macedonia. Macedonian prices are exceptionally cheap, particularly fruit and fresh vegetables.

I treat myself to chickpeas, gloves, pants and socks and eat in restaurants for the first time since Turkey.

PANAGITSA

This town only has a population of 400.

My host and his younger sisters run Children's Orchard School. They grow crops in summer and study in winter. WOW!

The children pay two euros a week to subsidise the selling of herbs against the purchase of cooking ingredients from Edessa, also saving for a microscope to start a science class.

I present my project and answer many questions.

EDESSA

I am in Edessa - a beautiful and hidden Greek treasure. WOW!

Edessa means *water tower* and is famous for waterfalls.

As the birthplace of the Macedonian kingdom, there are several tombs of kings.

A tranquil and serene fog falls on Mount Edessa while its scenery compensates for the hardship of cycling uphill in driving rain.

Cherries, peaches and walnuts grow here, harvested in June. There is also evidence all-around of the thriving cotton industry.

I hear the fifty-metre waterfall with its strange rock formation, made more magnificent by the torrent rainfall.

Walking behind the waterfall, I view Edessa and pause to reflect on the glory and strength of the cascading water, as it feeds the local power plant and nearby industrial cities like Gianitsa before flowing to Thessaloniki and on into the Aegean Sea. WOW!

THESSALONIKI

I consider Thessaloniki to be the best place in Greece, inspired by the *Open House* event where historical buildings are open to the public. I visit fifteen in two days and want to introduce this event to Korea. WOW!

A Greek lady, who attends my seminar, shares poetry to recite during my trip. The *Seikilos* epitaph is the world's oldest surviving musical composition.

While you live, shine.
Have no grief at all.
Life exists only for a short while
and time demands its due.

STAVROS

There are many vineyards on the way to Stavros, a gorgeous village beside the Aegean Sea.

I eat *Fasolya* giant beans with my hosts. The husband describes an impressive 2,600km bike ride from Hamburg to Stavros in aid of domestic violence and abused children. WOW!

KAVALA

I fall in love with the imposing city walls and the impressive port with its pretty harbour lights. Everything looks so much better when the sun replaces rain, grey sky changes to blue, and seagulls make their familiar cooing sound.

From the city walls, I watch as the sunrise sharpens and turns houses honey-coloured.

THASSOS

I take a ferry from Kavala to Thassos. I am so tired that I fall asleep. Without WiFi or signal, I can rest without distraction - simply sit back and relax in peace. WOW! My host accompanies me on a night walk, made challenging by bracing weather.

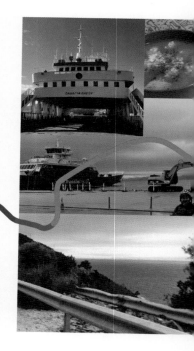

Apostle Paul is said to stop here on route from Troas to Philippi.

XANTHI

Xanthi is known as the city of a thousand colours. Like Komotini, there is a large population of Turkish-speaking Muslims dating back centuries to the Ottoman period.

A local Turk helps to ward off a gipsy, intent on harassing me.

KOMOTINI

I stay in a student dorm at Komotini University, eating with the students in the cafeteria.

I am surprised to see so many dogs in and around campus, even where we dine. WOW!

ALEXANDROUPOLI

Alexandroupoli is one of the few Greek cities with excellent bike paths. Athens does not have such things. WOW!

Decorative balconies are common in Greece.

The first thing I do is head for the Agean Sea. The landscapes differ dependent on the country. Here, there is a distant island with an enormous mountain surrounded by clouds.

I stay with a biology student who shows me her laboratory in the university hospital. We dance zumba, join a discussion, and photograph each other climbing trees.

MALKARA

There are so many hills on the way to Malkara! I use my downward momentum to get uphill. WOW!

I devour my packed lunch of goat and Kasar cheese, olives, eggs and bread in a border cafe, while the owner pours endless cups of tea and I watch spectacular flocks of blackbirds.

TEKIRDAG

Tekirdag is famous for agriculture, mainly wheat and *canola* rapeseed. The multi-family houses seem more creative and sophisticated by comparison to other Turkish cities.

Walking by the Marmara Sea late at night, I observe the crashing waves under the bright stars.

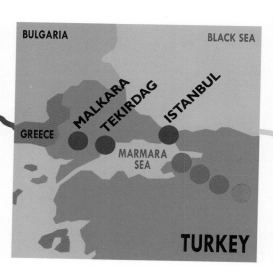

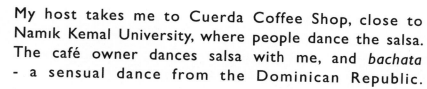

My host takes me to Cuerda Coffee Shop, close to Namık Kemal University, where people dance the salsa. The café owner dances salsa with me, and *bachata* - a sensual dance from the Dominican Republic.

I eat *ashure* porridge, also known as *Noah's pudding*, made with grains, dried fruits and nuts. Reputedly the world's oldest dessert, legend says that Noah concocted this from leftovers after weeks on the ark. WOW!

ISTANBUL

I visit **The Museum of Innocence**, fittingly the title of a book I am reading by **Orhan Pamuk** and a neat conclusion to my story of Turkey.

I participate in the *Fun Run* alongside the annual marathon, luckily a more modest walk or run of eight kilometres. Bosphorous Bridge, significantly spanning Asia and Europe and usually closed to pedestrians, is a great motivator. WOW!

It is so much fun to see so many people participating, either taking part and many women wearing hijabs, or spectating, cheering, playing music and picnicking.

"The future of museums is inside our own homes."
Orhan Pamuk

GEMLIK

I stay in a summer villa by the Sea of Marmara and meet my host's family and neighbours.

I eat anchovies and fried fish with chips and a green salad, sprinkled with tasty onions and olive oil, and washed down with a cold beer. WOW!

I wake early to see the big blue sea, spotting a bench in the yard and ladder access to the water.

BLACK SEA

GEMLIK
BURSA
INEGÖL

MARMARA
SEA

TURKEY

BURSA

Learning about Ottoman Empire towns, I visit a pretty village named Cumalıkızık, founded more than seven hundred years ago.

I love the grapevines, pastel-tone houses, the water flowing down from the mountain, the delicately swaying sound of the wooden chimes, and the smell of burning firewood.

I gorge on *Paynier* cheese and *Gözleme* aubergine filled flatbreads for lunch.

INEGÖL

Inegöl is a small city with a population of 250,000, famous for manufacturing plywood furniture.

I meet an agent responsible for sourcing furniture from the hundreds of companies, and for negotiating competitive prices for his clients.

Visiting a pastry shop, established by a local craftsman in 1990, I sample sweet, sticky, fenugreek seed *Helba* cake.

Inegöl is a conservative city with no bars, only selling beer in a hotel.

I attend a Turkish wedding. The bride and groom, both dressed in blue, dance to Turkish Arabic music, joined by friends of the bride and watched by guests sat on plastic chairs who appear indifferent as if viewing a boring television programme. WOW!

Young boys and girls run around eating snacks, surrounded by more than two hundred women, mostly wearing hijabs.

I make sketches of the feast and the children.

ESKIŞEHIR

Eskişehir translates as *the old city* where, fortunately, newer modern buildings have not yet replaced the traditional nineteenth-century houses.

I visit *Sazova Park* and its lovely lake, castle, and zoo.

A glassmaker gives me a pendant of *Nazar Boncugu* - the Turkish blue-eyed talisman to overcome disaster.

I experience a delicious and hearty Turkish breakfast while watching the tranquil Porsuk River. WOW!

BLACK SEA

ESKIŞEHIR

POLATLI

ANKARA

GÖREME

TURKEY

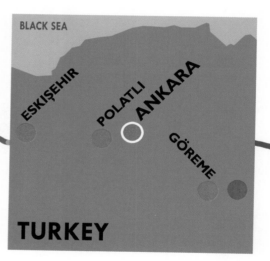

POLATLI

Common local crops are wheat, onions and chickpeas.

I stay with a family on top of a hill, where the husband is a soldier, and the wife is a wheat engineer at the agriculture research centre.

"Wheat is the most productive crop," she tells me, *"so we study* **sunn** *wheat pests. If we know our enemies, we can fight better!"*

ANKARA

Ankara is the capital city of Turkey. I coincide with *Turkish National Day* and visit the *Atatürk Memorial* with two university students, surrounded by locals waving Turkish flags and portraits of *Kemal Atatürk*, the founding father of the Republic of Turkey in 1923.

I stay with a journalist reporting on current autocratic actions. I read *2016 - Present Purges in Turkey* to gain a greater understanding of the situation.

GÖREME

I buy a tent to detour across several mountains, cycling uphill 1700 metres for two days, and enduring driving rain and 3° cold in my summer jacket.

I fulfil a personal ambition and visit Kapadokya in the heart of Turkey, famous for unique geological features called *fairy chimneys* and amazing hot-air balloons.

I witness the most beautiful sunrises and hot air balloons floating up into the dark skies, illuminated by their fuel like Christmas lights. The surreal peaceful landscape of pale blues, purples and pinks makes the perfect backdrop to watch the balloons head west, surpassing expectations. WOW!

In Göreme, I stay in a house built into a cave with an adorable bedroom, kitchenette, and bathroom.

KAYSERI

My hosts invite me to a café to play a traditional Turkish board game called *Tulan*, similar to *Yutnori* in Korea.

After drinking Turkish coffee, my host thrills me by reading my fortune from the dregs. It is like being in Professor Trelawney's witch class in Harry Potter. WOW!

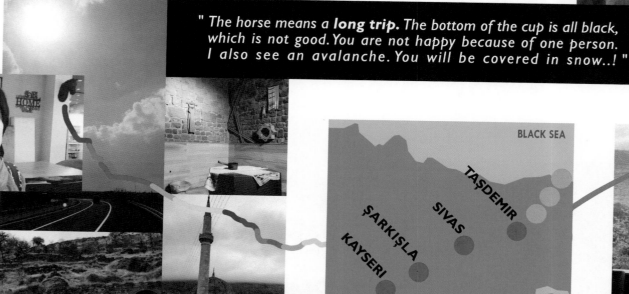

" *The horse means a **long trip.** The bottom of the cup is all black, which is not good. You are not happy because of one person. I also see an avalanche. You will be covered in snow..!* "

TURKEY

BLACK SEA

TAŞDEMIR

SIVAS

ŞARKIŞLA

KAYSERI

ŞARKIŞLA

Şarkışla is a medium-sized city, not big enough to have *Warmshower hosts,* and not so small to have generous locals to invite me for tea.

So I must stay in a hotel.

SIVAS

I have a body massage at *Kurşunlu Hamamı* Turkish bathhouse. Unlike Korea, the masseur rubs and washes my head like she is using a scrubber to remove dirt from a potato.

Also performing headlocks, she enjoys my short hair and makes it rise like a lit candle. Luckily, unlike Korea, it is a massage with a smile. WOW!

TAŞDEMIR **Cycling through the mountains, I decide to buy vegetables from an organic store.**

Placing my bike on the stall, I spot a couple drinking tea on a nearby farm. They invite me to join, handing me a fork so that I can also eat with them. It becomes too dark to cycle, so they insist that I dine and sleep at their house.

Thanking Allah for sending me, the lady supplies much appreciated warm clothes and a hijab for my hair. In the morning, we milk the cow, which makes my fingers smell cheesy. It reminds me of Thomas Hardy's *Tess*. The lady pours some milk into a *Peinir* bowl to make cheese and heats the rest to pasteurise for drinking.

There is nothing like drinking fresh cow's milk. WOW!

TORUL

Cycling up the Pontic Mountains to a height of 1844 metres is extremely tough. I only hear my panting and the sound of a small creek flowing towards the Black Sea. I am okay alone, cycling up the never-ending hills in the strong sunlight, spurred on to reach the Kapadokya region. Five restaurants give me chai and dessert. A truckdriver offers a lift, but I decline, replying, *"Sorun değil,"* which is Turkish for *no problem.* I set small targets to help reach the top. I breathe a sigh of relief and head down to stay at a petrol station before sunset.

MAÇKA

The Sumela Monastery is closed at the top of the Pontic Mountains. Disappointed, I cycle down the treacherous roads to a bike-themed café. I order one dish, but the owner serves more, including *Dolmas* stuffed vine leaves with rice. Then her mother kindly invites me to stay at her house. WOW!

BLACK SEA · GEORGIA · TRABZON · HOPA · RIZE · MAÇKA · TORUL · TURKEY

TRABZON

I enjoy the city museum, learning that the region is famous for *Peyniri* string cheese, and *Horon* group folk dancing. Next day, I am lucky enough to eat Peyniri for breakfast and to watch locals dancing Horon in a café!

I climb to the top of Boztepe hill to view Trabzon from above. WOW!

Jianan and I depart ways. I continue alone.

RIZE

Turkish chai tea comes from this area. I stay above a famous café where Turkish men play *Okey*, a tile-based game, played by four players.

HOPA

I come across a little house by the coast where cyclists stop for tea or to stay the night, and inscribe messages on its outside wall.

I am delighted to write the first Korean words.

I meet the owner, and two Iranians who perform traditional Iranian dances in costume, determined to spread, *more dance, less war,* in every city they visit. It is compelling. WOW!

BATUMI

The vibrant scene from my window is full of striking pastel tones. As I prepare to leave, I reminisce how pleasant, pretty and joyful Georgia is to cycle.

UREKI

Aided by good weather and stunning scenery, I arrive at the Black Sea three weeks after the Caspian Sea.

The Black Sea has fine black sand which feels fantastic on the feet. I read and watch the sunset, reminded of hongsi as the reducing *red door* disappears, replaced by a silver crescent moon.

I am delighted to have Khachapuri once more.

As I stare across the Black Sea, my Khachapuri egg resembles the sun, and its bread a boat, symbolic and poetic.

Like the Azari region, I rip off the *bow* to mix the yolk and cheese, then cut like a pizza.

Delicious with tomato-cucumber salad. WOW!

SAMTREDIA

I stay at an impressive two-story house on top of a hill with an extensive garden and a spectacular view.

My hosts gift me sweet homemade wine.

I stop at a fruit stand to buy *hongsi*, a name given by Koreans to Asian persimmon when it is exceedingly ripe and perfectly squishy. WOW!

ZESTAFONI

A local man offers his house. Every meal is a *supra* traditional Georgian feast where the *tamada* makes a toast. The longer and more meaningful, the better!

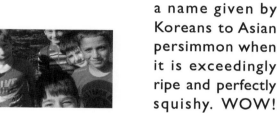

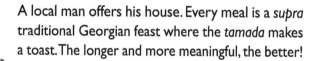

"Let's celebrate family. When the family is healthy, all aspects of a person are healthy."

Zestafoni is famous for mushrooms. I have grilled mushrooms with *Khachapuri*, a traditional Georgian bread dish containing cheese, eggs and other ingredients with its crust for dipping.

GORI **I see the Gori Fortress, a medieval citadel on a rocky hill above Gori.**

Georgia is a beautiful and picturesque country. Notably its autumn landscapes and the medieval mountain villages between Gori and Zestafoni.

TBILISI

I stay seven days in this fascinating capital city.

I treat myself to two Georgian baths, soaking in hot sulphur said to benefit skin, immunity and circulation.

Chreli-Abano is a beautiful bathhouse with an iconic tiled mosque-like façade, and where I select a *kisi* traditional exfoliation treatment.

The attendant scrubs my body vigorously with a textured mitt ridding dead skin, then washes away with a foamy pillow. I feel like I am in heaven - it is a miraculous experience. WOW!

I sample Saperavi and Kveveri wine.

Saperavi is an acidic grape native to a well-known winemaking region.

Kveveri is the name of the clay vessel into which freshly squeezed grape juice is poured and then buried in the ground to ferment.

I am lucky to catch *Tbilisoba*, an October festival that celebrates the diversity and history of Tbilisi.

I enjoy eating grilled meat in the hustle and bustle of Old Tbilisi.

Surrounded by stalls filled with hundreds of harvest products from different regions of Georgia.

Georgia's famous male choir sings every Sunday morning in Kvashveti Cathedral, where women must wear long trousers or over-the-knee skirts, and always cover their heads with scarves.

I listen for an hour and marvel at their glorious harmonies. WOW!

TOVUZ

I try *Warmshowers* for the first time, a specialist website for cyclists to find local hosts around the world.

My host greets me with a lunch of *Toyuq Sousu* chicken and potato. I shed tears eating spicy red pepper!

For dinner, my host cooks *Khingal* dumplings, sprinkled with an agreeable combination of what tastes like live yoghurt and tomato. WOW!

I also eat dry bread with butter and cheese. It is so dry that it preserves up to two weeks.

My host takes
me to a vineyard
where I pick as many grapes as I can,
navigating my way through maze-like vines.
The juice makes my hands sticky and purple!

GANJA

Ganja is Azerbaijan's second-largest city, full of cobblestones, towering mosques, and houses made from red bricks. I stay in a hostel in the old town situated on Javad Khan Street, the traditional shopping street.

Ganja is the birthplace of the famous poet, Nizami Ganjavi, whose children's book, *Seven Beauties*, I read as a child.

YEVLAX

I stay in an old house with a cow barn, a chicken cage and a pomegranate garden. Azerbaijan homes appear to have typical layouts and habits. Every yard has a table with a plastic cover, and a sink to wash fruit, vegetables and your teeth!

Before dinner, everyone drinks tea with honey-dipped berries served in glass holders, all with different designs and coupled with glass containers full of *must-have* sugar and candy.

The wooden door entrances often have white lace curtains which are lovely to touch.

UJAR

I study the houses on my morning walk. They are good size with two stories and a big yard. Their delicate rooves resemble traditional Asian except that they are steel instead of wood. Intriguingly, there are stars, roses and trees inscribed into the upper stories, and pomegranates protrude from every wall and hang on every fence. Pomegranates are everywhere. WOW!

KURDAMIR

The Azerbaijans show friendship and warmth wherever I go.

A street vendor kindly hands me some melon as I cycle past. The majority of cars seek my attention to wave encouragement. A busload of people hangs out of the windows to cheer me on.

HAJIGABUL

I encounter a man in a restaurant whom, without warning and uninvited, tries to hug and kiss me on the cheek. I make my feelings known and he retreats. WOW!

BAKU

Baku is a beautiful city. The Azerbaijan men are very handsome and sound so cute when they speak. I walk through the old city and its ancient fortress to see the *Maiden's Tower* and the statue of *Aliagha Vahid*, an Azerbaijani poet, with past and present Azerbaijan figures carved into a giant head.

A *concert* unfolds in the common room when a few sailors begin to sing and play.

I capture their passion in my sketchbook and reminisce about all the brilliant things I am leaving behind as I start the next phase of my journey, arriving into Baku, the capital city of Azerbaijan.

KAZAKHSTAN

AKTAU

CASPIAN SEA

BAKU

AZERBAIJAN

MEMORIES OF BAKU

- Red glass pomegranate souvenirs for sale in artisan markets
- Flame towers depicting the three colours of the Azerbaijan flag
- Walking along the Caspian Sea coastline in the cool breeze
- Drinking Azerbaijan tea with lemon in an *armudu* pear-shaped glass

The Caspian Sea is 125 metres dee

AKTAU

Leaving Kazakhstan, I cross the Caspian Sea by ferry. Due to rough weather, the twenty-four-hour journey now takes thirty-six! I gain strength from my fellow cyclists and befriend the captain's assistant. He informs me that the ferry's name is *Professor Gru* after a prominent Azerbaijan geographer and sea captain who calculated the depths of the Caspian Sea during the 1910s. We reflect how, as travellers, we are all sailors of a sort, navigating *the sea of life*.

At night I stargaze and spot a shooting star. The sailors tell me how they work four-hour shifts in the engineering room where it can reach temperatures as high as 55°C. WOW!

The trainride from Taraz to Aktau takes an incredible forty-eight hours.

Unlike Chinese trains where cup noodles are commonplace, the Kazakhs erect small tables to eat their homemade meals of bread, cakes and biscuits, with some diners stretching to cucumbers, tomatoes and eggs. It is a veritable feast. WOW!

TARAZ

I meet a Kazakh-Korean middle-aged gentleman, who, unlike his father, cannot speak any Korean!

He has a Russian wife and three children and owns a local supermarket, a café and even a nightclub.

A local celebrity, his friends and customers greet and initiate conversations as he walks down the street.

Every afternoon, I take a break from work and go for a short walk.

I appear to be the only person wearing sunglasses and a hat and covering my arms from the sun. WOW!

People give me strange glances, thinking that I must be a tourist.

One fine afternoon, I parade through green leafy trees and perform simple breathing exercises. It helps to free my mind as I inhale and exhale deep and slow, assisted by the calming streets of Taraz.

I visit the Aisha-Bibi Mausoleum dating back to the eleventh or twelfth-century, with its intricate and decorative patterns.

A man named Karakhan built the mausoleum in memory of his love for Aisha-Bibi, a local noblewoman who died young from a snakebite and whose father disapproved of their love.

In a local Korean restaurant, I read a great book about the Koreans of Kazakhstan, telling the story of many thousands of Koreans escaping famine, poverty, and Japanese colonial oppression between the 1860s and the 1930s. They live in dug-outs, ordered to grow rice in the *Kazakh Steppe*, a vast open grassland located in northern Kazakhstan adjacent to Russia.

I stay in Taraz for one week to catch up on work, deciding to take a train close to the Kazakhstan border because it will take too long to cycle the month-long journey before Jianan's visa expires.

KULAN

A shepherd crosses the road with over a hundred sheep, pounding the ground and raising dust.

I stop to buy magical fruit at the fruit shop. Blue, oval, and delicious, they turn out to be plums! I buy twenty for next to no money.

Then men, standing in front of a large blue truck containing bees, beckon me over to taste from their yellow honey bucket. It is very sweet, and I can discern the sugary grains. WOW!

SHU

Shu has one cinema. It requires an audience of at least four people before it plays a movie. I try four times during the day, but each time it falls short, and I cannot watch the film!

MERKI

Merki is a beautiful neighbourhood with tall trees, and houses elegantly painted in mint and turquoise.

The majority of local drivers slow down to wave and to encourage as they pass by. It helps me to pedal faster.

KOKKAYNAR

This region is home to Turks only. A generous man invites me to stay in his house and refuses any money before he prepares a hot bath and a sauna. His young wife is pregnant with their second child and wears an ankle-length dress, a long grey cardigan, and wraps her hair in a pink scarf.

Like a heaven-sent *Good Samaritan*, she is kind and cooks *bosh*, a dish with potatoes and cabbage, similar in taste to *kimchi-jjigae* and accompanied by tasty pickled peppers and an olive salad. We finish with homegrown watermelon - very crunchy and sweet, which they typically export to Russia.

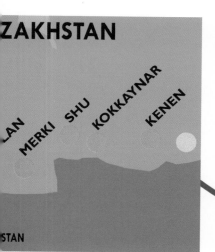

KENEN

Arriving to stay at a Kazakh family house, the husband introduces me to his wife. She has pale skin and Asian features.

Then he introduces me to another woman, much younger and with darker skin applying makeup, who turns out to be his girlfriend!

The wife serves tomato and cucumber salad with four types of meat, and fried fish, accompanied by raisins, candy and bread.

She boils freshly gathered milk and hands me a bowl, demonstrating how to tear the bread and to soak in the warm, savoury milk.

It tastes delicious. WOW!

UZYNAGASH   The waitresses wear aprons with front pockets tied by ribbons behind their waists. They wear a towel on their head and have an x-shaped slipper on their socks. The stiff plastic tablecloths have floral or character patterns, serving slightly tough bread, tea with sugar and a reused bottle of vodka housing vinegar in its body and salt in its lid. WOW!

ALMATY   A group of children surround me. A young girl, fairytale-like in a traditional blouse, says in English, *"Come with us! We want to invite you to our home."* I find it impossible to decline when they plead all so innocently and cutely!

I go with ten others in a car, and stay with her family - three generations, totalling twelve living in a house with a large garden and a sauna.

We eat Pilaf rice dish for lunch and dinner.

KAZAKHSTAN

UZYNAGASH
ALMATY

KYRGYZSTAN   CHINA

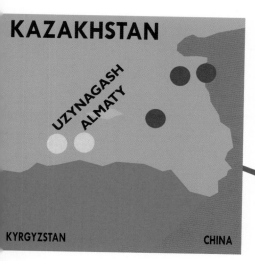

The mother wears a hijab and a long dress, in which she also dresses me. The children, well educated and learning boxing, are able to play *Tembur*, a string instrument. They appear happy and free when compared with a similar family in China. The eldest son teaches me the Russian alphabet.

Korea and Kazakhstan have common history. Escaping famine, poverty and Japanese oppression, 180,000 Koreans settle in the Russian territories between 1860 and 1930. They are deported to Central Asia in Stalin's 1937 ethnic cleansing.

My new Korean friend's family invite me to a Korean dinner. The parents describe how hard it was for the grandparents - expelled to Central Asia, and stripped of their home and assets to make their way up again through hard work.

A story of struggle they recount as a reminder.

I meet a Korean on a bus. He invites me to visit Kok Tobe mountain and buys me an Almaty fridge magnet. The view from the cable car is stunning. I find a *big apple* statue.

Almaty is the second biggest Kazakhstan city whose name *Alma-Ata* means *father of apples* in Kazakh, claiming to be the birthplace of the apple for more than a hundred years.

Chinese chicken stew, *Dapanji*, is also eaten in Kazakhstan.

CHUNDZHA

Farmers use sturdy donkeys to carry their heavy loads. The Kazakhstans are super friendly, greeting me as I cycle past, even slowing down in their cars to cruise at my pace. WOW!

The roads are worn out and patched together like repaired clothes, making them difficult to ride, and in need of my ultra-tight sports bra once more! At night we experience two power cuts.

ZHARKENT

Arriving at dawn, I witness Kazakhstan women sweeping the yards, and merchants in full swing preparing for market as fresh fruit is delivered. I eat meat pies, porridge, milky tea, and egg and ham for a hearty and affordable breakfast.

Local boys invite me to an eighteenth birthday party. I am pleasantly surprised by their turnout. The boys attend wearing smart clothing and neat hair while one of the girls sports a see-through blouse! They do not drink alcohol, consuming iced tea and cola, one by one standing to toast the birthday boy.

I ask the boys about their dreams - one wants a good job and to be the happiest person in the world, one aspires to be a teacher, one hopes to go to an American University, and one aims to be a soldier.

I meet a Moroccan cycling on a solar-powered bicycle from Lyon in France to Guangzhou in China.

He informs me that the Kazakhstans are the most friendly of the eleven countries he has visited, but he refuses to camp in Kazakhstan because of the snakes. WOW!

KHORGOS

Sayram Lake is charming and peaceful with ethnic minorities living in yurts, riding horses and savouring the vegetation.

I smell the wildflowers and internet search their names. Unfortunately, when I horse ride in the meadow, my horse has a mind of its own, taking me through pine trees and scratching my face and legs. Ouch. WOW!

KAZAKHSTAN

CHUNDZHA

ZHARKENT KHORGOS

KYRGYZSTAN

CHINA

I arrive at the bus terminal to bid farewell to China and board the special bus to cross into Kazakhstan.

ÜRÜMQI

It is my impression that western China is kinder and more welcoming than eastern China, possibly being remote and further from the main cities like Beijing and Shanghai.

Xinjiang province is famous for lamb meat and *Zhuafan*, a dish made of lamb, rice, carrot and yellow radish. I taste the most delicious lamb meat in Ürümqi. WOW!

TURPAN

I am impressed with Jiaohe, a ruined city and a UNESCO-designated cultural heritage site, situated above the plateau in Turpan. From afar, it looks like a single cave, but as I approach, Jiaohe is a city full of caves. Mind-blowing. WOW!

I befriend a girl from my hostel. We walk through the alleys of the ancient city and memorise a poem.

As if camels cross the town,
I hear a camel bell in voices of crowds.
In marketplace still busy as it was,
Wagons form a flowing water, and horses a dragon.
Nonetheless, the royal palace of luxury
Has become a piece of ruins.
A thousand years of delights and sorrows marking each meeting and farewell
No longer leaves its trail.
Men whose life still last shall live to the fullest,
But shall not expect the earth to cherish their memories.

Translation: Jungmin Lee

I witness the pride and wisdom of the Xinjiang people, who survived for a thousand years expanding their cave network one under another.

I taste the grapes hanging all over the valley in Turpan, and see the largest oven in the world that makes *nang*, a special flatbread of the area.

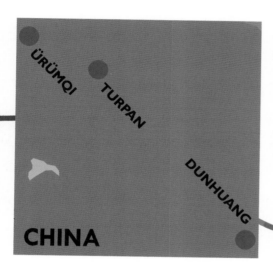

ÜRÜMQI

TURPAN

DUNHUANG

CHINA

DUNHUANG

Dunhuang is an oasis at a religious and cultural crossroads on the Silk Road. I ride an electric scooter across the uninhabited sand dunes, and following Korean tradition when one climbs a mountain, shout my wish across the vast desert.

I visit the Mogao Caves containing some of the finest examples of Buddhist art spanning a thousand years. I write peacefully in the light of a dark yellow cave in front of a Buddha statue. Most tourists glimpse and go, but the Buddha keeps me calm and without fear, stimulating me to embrace this peace of mind. Western cathedrals can be overwhelming while eastern grottoes invoke a humble feeling of tranquillity and love.

LANZHOU

I try *Sanpaotai*, the favourite local tea, its name deriving from the three-part composition of tea lid, tea bowl and tea saucer. Tradition is to pick up the saucer, scrape the tea leaves with the lid then drink from the big bowl, flavouring with dried dates, rock sugar, roses, lychees, raisins and chrysanthemums.

The locals are very hospitable, offering dinner, listening to my stories and suggesting local tourist activities which is very helpful.

I stay with the owner of Lihong's restaurant. One of her chefs teaches me how to cook my favoured dinner choice *Gong Bao Ji Ding - Sichuan Kung Pao Chicken*, a famous and simple-looking Chinese dish, or so I thought!

Surrounded by the buzz of twelve chefs helping and encouraging each other, I slice the scallions - young green onions, but too thin!

So I stand back and observe the mastery as the chef snaps the pan on the fire, combines chicken, peanuts, scallions, and a variety of nine seasonings including pepper, salt and sugar to create this tastiest of dishes in a matter of moments. It is fascinating and mouth-watering to watch. WOW!

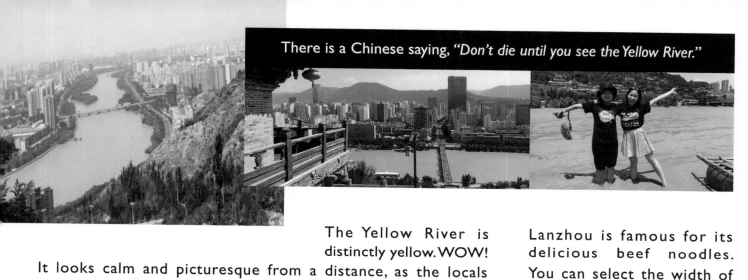

There is a Chinese saying, *"Don't die until you see the Yellow River."*

The Yellow River is distinctly yellow. WOW!

It looks calm and picturesque from a distance, as the locals play cards and drink tea before meals, erecting parasols and deck chairs by the river. I feel the pureness of the water and the soft, fine sand beneath my feet.

Lanzhou is famous for its delicious beef noodles. You can select the width of the noodles, ranging from *capillary* thin to *leek leaf* wide.

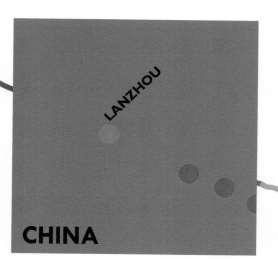

LANZHOU

CHINA

Go to Lanzhou and order beef noodle with a pile of meat. You will thank me!

I decide to rest in Lanzhou before taking a train through Xinjiang Province, unwilling to risk its vast desert.

I send ahead my bicycle and luggage to Khorgos at the China Kazakhstan border.

YUZHONG

Finding a place to camp is not easy. I try a large farm with a small reservoir, but the grumpy farmer sends me away, so I go back to the top of the hill and find an ideal spot. I flatten the weeds and pitch the tent, where finally, I can rest my weary head. Heaven. WOW!

DINGXI

The altitude is 2300 metres above sea level, and the temperature is seventeen degrees even though it is the start of August. The cold weather forces me to wear a jumper. Then it starts to rain. Fine spray covers my face when large trucks pass. I hear nothing but the sound of my bike riding over the rain-drenched roads. I begin to worry as I cycle through the mountains - fearing that something goes wrong and I get stuck. I keep pedalling.

TONGWEI

This section of the highway is desolate and exhausting. There are only mountains, roads and cars, and no place to rest. The ants crawl over my body when I sit beside the road. I want to escape the fast and threatening vehicles, and the squashed roadkill strewn along the way.

TIANSHUI

I am dumbfounded by the scale of China when I visit Maiji mountain in Tianshui, more so than when I visited the *Terracotta Warriors* or the *Forbidden City*. I am amazed by the gigantic figure of Buddha carved into the rock which appears *stern* when the guide turns on the light and *crying* when the guide turns off the light. WOW!

I love that Buddhism examples are close to nature.

It rains heavily, and clouds begin to rise from the wet forest.

DONGCHA

Unsuccessful in finding accommodation in resident homes, I find the cheapest hotel of my trip at only seven euros a night. WOW!

I pass a young girl holding a basket of *jujube* date-like fruit who invites me to her house. Her yard is full of *huajiao* Sichuan pepper with its refreshing aroma, which I taste before she hands me a bag.

It has a hot and intense flavour.

YUZHONG

DINGXI

TONGWEI

TIANSHUI

DONGCHA

CHINA

BAOJI

The farms and houses look peaceful. It is early afternoon when I arrive at a bike shop to repair my rear tyre. Suddenly, it starts to pour. The bike shop owner watches while his wife and son wash their faces in the rainwater flowing through the canopy holes. It shocks me a little as they keep washing their hands and collecting rain in a basin before returning inside for lunch!

ZHOUZHI

Red peppers are drying in the sun. Alongside, there are peach flowers and a cornfield. I enter the supermarket to avoid the sun - the first supermarket that only accepts cash, neither mobile payments nor credit cards. WOW!

The sun and the clouds turn pink. I cross the bridge and stop to capture the scene. The river water is clean, reflecting the landscape.

XI'AN

I return briefly before continuing my cycling route.

YAN'AN

Acting as a *red tourist*, I detour to Yan'an, the Communist Party's revolutionary base for twelve years. The city is full of university students, and company workers wearing similar T-shirts.

I travel on a bus to Liangjiahe, a village about seventy miles from Yan'an. The current Chinese leader, Xi Jinping, is sent here at fifteen by Mao Zedong, the post World War II revolutionist leader, as part of a campaign to force the educated urban youth to live a peasant's life.

Xi Jinping spent seven years as a hard labourer, ploughing fields, carrying manure, caring for sheep and turning the millstone with a donkey. He slept on a flea-ridden straw mat but found solace reading books. The experience taught him how to serve the people, and the village rallied to send him to Tsinghua University in Beijing in 1975.

"Liangjiahe formed many of my ideas and characteristics," Xi said in 2004.

I visit a small room in one of the hillside cave dwellings where Xi stayed. It has drinking flasks, agricultural tools and posters of Mao. I get a taste of teenage life and the state of mind of those sent to the countryside during the Cultural Revolution, and I ponder whether everyone can learn from such an experience.

WEEKS 5,6,7   XI'AN

I visit the Consulate General for the Republic of Korea, and enter through a secret door, passing several pictures of Korea and into a large, elegant room. The Consul General listens as I describe my cycling trip, and says, *"It is a very topical and meaningful trip. The strength of Korean youth is their language proficiency, their creativity, and their appetite for adventure."*

I meet iFeng's journalist, who shows me around the Small Wild Goose Tower. I strike the Qin Dynasty bell, which dates back to 1192. The loud, clear sound resonates over a five-kilometre radius. In China, they ring the bell during the day and beat the drum at night.

I ring the bell nine times and love the heavy feeling of the striking clapper as it vibrates up my arm and through my entire body. WOW!

TEN STRANGE SHAANXI PROVINCE CUSTOMS
- Noodles as wide as belts • Pancakes as big as pan covers • *Paomo* breadcrumb stew sold in big bowls
- Entire dishes made of delicious *capsicum* peppers • Bowls as big as basins • Roaring operatic singing
- Handkerchief headdresses • Half-built houses • Girls that marry locally • Everyone squatting on stools

长安梦 CHANG'AN IMPRESSIONS

Chang'an Impressions is a live performance which takes place on the City Wall. It is a well-organized performance of costume, dance and composition.

The women's dance stands out more than the soldier's. The soldiers have fixed expressions to represent bravery, while the women express beauty with every gesture and make me think, "These women are awake," as I observe their animated eyes even when they are static for long periods.

It is funny to watch the performers pack up their belongings after the show and exit using their mobile phones. One minute, they are pretending to be from the Tang dynasty, the next they are back in the present - as if time travelling.

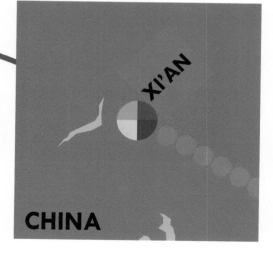

XI'AN

CHINA

While Jianan flies back to Shanghai to obtain several visas, I stay for three weeks painting *China Promenade* to depict my cycling trip from Shanghai to Xi'an.

I also gain certification in **coffee-hand-dripping** after completing a ten class course.

LANTIAN

Everyone sells tofu and potatoes in baskets, which reminds me of Korea and Gangwon-do's high-altitude farming. I cycle Qing Ling mountain, 1200 metres above sea level. It is an impressive rock formation as if outlined with a brush pen that adds to its intensity. As I cycle down to Lantian, the air warms and I miss the more refreshing atmosphere. I look back and thank Qing Ling for allowing me to pass.

SHANGLUO

The Shaanxi scenery looks so mysterious on a rainy day as the mountains appear more rugged and picturesque. My sneakers get wet and heavy, so I decide to cycle in slippers. The rain drenches my head as it finds its way through the holes in my helmet.

DANFENG

I go rafting on a banana boat down the Dan River. However, the wind is blowing backwards, so we have to row. The water is not the cleanest, but I end up diving deep. I lay on the boat looking up at the sky and the sedimentary geography, watching the clouds move at different heights.

Unlike lying on grass, the boat's movement makes me feel like I am flying. WOW!

SHANGNAN

I leave Henan Province and pain! I am sure there will be more dirt roads, but for now, I am delighted to bid farewell. No more tighter-fitting sports bras for the bumpy ride!

The Shaanxi Province houses are rustic, and the streets are immaculate.

XIXIA

There are many houses with roses, sunflowers, and the *Rose of Sharon*, the national flower of Korea, making their gardens look lovely.

Interesting fact: during the Cultural Revolution, Chinese people picked all the flowers. WOW!

LANTIAN
SHANGLUO
DANFENG
SHANGNAN
XIXIA
NEIXIANG

CHINA

NEIXIANG

I cycle by a statue of Zhang Zhongjing, a famous doctor from China who also had a significant influence on Korea and Japan.

Learning from other doctors, Zhang Zhongjing developed different theories, methods and remedies, prescribing and healing many.

Folklore says that when Zhang Zhongjing made *Jiaozi* Chinese dumpling, he wrapped lamb, pepper, and herbs in flour dumplings, then put them in boiling water to make dumpling soup, curing those with frostbite.

NANYANG

Nanyang has a developing cattle industry. The cows look happy and healthy, as I pass a shepherd herding his sheep. On my way to the supermarket, I see that everyone has a sheep in front of their house. They make great lawnmowers! From the rooftop, I observe vast fertile fields and pastures. Agriculture plays a vital role in the economy, producing wheat for noodles, corn on the cob, and tobacco for cigarettes.

YANGCE

Two days of rain create muddy roads and muddy puddles! Cycling through my first puddle, I have no idea how deep it is. I get caught in the mud and fall off my bike. Covered in mud and with wet feet, I get up slowly by putting my hands in the dirty water. It is disgusting. WOW!

ZHUMADIAN

As I cycle in the rain, I get a puncture.

Changing the rear tyre in the rain is a harrowing experience, especially on the unsurfaced roads of the Henan Province as large trucks roar past. It is very dangerous. WOW!

PINGYU

The terrain is challenging and slow, but the scenery is captivating - the sort of landscape to inspire Van Gogh, with clouds resembling earthquakes in search of the sun's rosy fingers.

Although underdeveloped, there is something pure and familiar about this Chinese town and its inhabitants.

LINQUAN

Linquan is the most populous county in China. On the National Poor County List, it is excluded from paying tax. I visit the **K**orean **L**iberation **A**rmy training and recruiting site, which is now Linquan Middle School.

The KLA was formed in Chungking, China in 1940, by the Provisional Government of the Republic of Korea, and joined the allied side fighting in China and Southeast Asia in 1941.

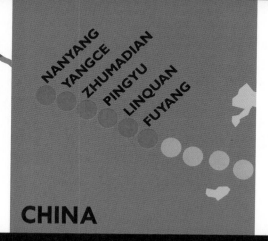

NANYANG
YANGCE
ZHUMADIAN
PINGYU
LINQUAN
FUYANG

FUYANG

An electric tricycle approaches on the wrong side of the road. We turn the same way and collide, leaving me with scratched ankles and a scratched bike.

Luckily, no serious injuries. It is a close call. WOW!

CHINA

FRIGHTFUL FACTS ABOUT FUYANG
Between 1959 and 1961, 2.4 million people die from famine
In the 1990s, commercial blood selling schemes lead to entire villages becoming infected with HIV
In 2004, a food scandal involving fake infant formula causes the death of 50–60 children

YINGSHANG

Anhui province is under development. Trucks, contraflows and construction sites are unavoidable. I have to hold my breath due to the asphalt, chalk powder and dust. When I arrive at the hotel, my face is black with dirt. The hotel is like something from a western movie or a desert in Arizona, USA, where I used to live when I was ten. WOW!

DINGYUAN

Cycling in soaring temperatures and with no shade gives me a headache and makes me dizzy when I remove my helmet. I realise for the first time the danger of sunstroke. I have food and medicine to make myself better.

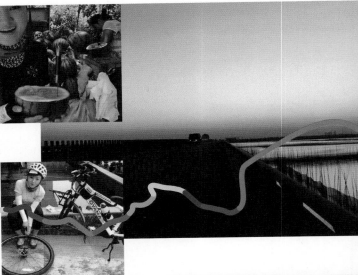

HUAINAN

My family name is Yoo (劉) in Chinese, Liu. My ancestors include Liu Bang, the founder of the Han dynasty as Emperor Gaozu of Han, and Liu Bei Warlord from the late Han Dynasty and founding emperor of Shu Han. Part of the Liu family moved to Korea one thousand years ago.

I see a tomb with the surname, *Liu* - the tomb of Liu An and grandson of Liu Bang, the founder of the Han Dynasty…and the inventor of soya milk. It is incredible to know that my ancestors invented tofu, one of my favourite foods. WOW!

ZHULONG

Anhui province has many scenic points and is full of nature. At sunset, the strawberry fields turn to gold. It is very serene. Zhulong is a small and delightful town. As the first foreigner to visit, the police twice check my identity in my hotel room. They ask to take a *selfie*. It is problematic for foreigners to stay in budget hotels in China.

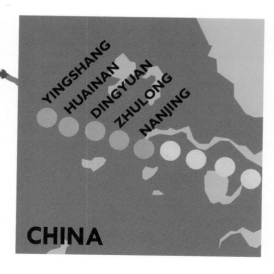

YINGSHANG HUAINAN DINGYUAN ZHULONG NANJING

CHINA

NANJING

Nanjing is a charming city with a long history - six Chinese dynasties had their capital here.

The scenery from Yuejiang Tower is green and lush, and mountainous, unlike Shanghai. There is a mural depicting Zheng He's world travel, peacefully exploring some eighty-seven years earlier than Marco Polo, and bringing back magnificent animals like giraffes, elephants, and lions. Incidentally, the guide accuses the West of using Chinese-made explosives as a means of aggression!

WEEK I   SHANGHAI • KUNSHAN • WUXI • CHANGZHOU • DANYANG

DANYANG

Leaving Changzhou, I adore cycling beside the pink and white flowers and discovering more beautiful villages. One is called Yili with houses built around farms and ponds. People wear conical hats like in Vietnam. I see smoke coming from a farm. Although banned by the government, Chinese farmers burn the fields in June to clear the crop stalks after the harvest in preparation for planting.

CHANGZHOU

Changzhou has two big hotels that host the annual award ceremony, which my previous media company employers organise. Rather than taking a train from Shanghai to Changzhou, this time, I arrive on a bicycle, and visit the same restaurant - *Chocolate*. Tasty. WOW!

Chinese cities seem similar because I only eat lunch, stay in a hotel, then depart!

WUXI

Wuxi is a beautiful fishing town. I discover the wonderful sight of fishermen by the lake. I also see groups of young people riding rental *Hello Bikes*. It is lovely to see the Wuxi people live and fish close to the lake. I cycle along the river and pass many older men fishing from its banks. On leaving Wuxi, I stop to observe the grand theatre. It resembles a hawk gliding gracefully over the lake.

It is my 28th birthday. I eat noodles because, in China, people eat noodles on birthdays to symbolise longevity.

KUNSHAN

From Kunshan, I enjoy cycling through the Jiangsu province, rather flat and with stunning lakes. Kunshan is a city where many Taiwanese people live. I stay at my friend's house. The cycling lanes are cyclist-friendly, paved with delightful tiles and separated from pedestrians and vehicles by thick bushes.

SHANGHAI   I set off from Zhapu bridge with the best view of Shanghai's skyline.

"Goodbye, Pearl Tower! You attracted me to Shanghai, now you see me off."

PREPARATION

AMBITIONS AND GOALS

A   **Cycle and experience the changing landscape from Shanghai to London**

B   **Interview startup entrepreneurs from each country on the ancient Silk Road**

C   **Hold a seminar in the biggest city along the way**

MONEY

Eva spends 10,800 euro in 36 weeks - 300 euro a week, about 45 euro a day! A combination of credit card and local currency exchange bureaus.

VISAS AND IMMUNISATION

Given South Korean status, Eva only needs a visa for Azerbaijan, and already immunised, she requires no injections.

SPONSORSHIP

Eva finds fourteen sponsors from China, South Korea and Taiwan. The main sponsor is a Shanghai blockchain marketing company. Other sponsors range from a venture capitalist, and a travel startup to a learning academy and a translation company, some assisting with money and insurance, others providing essential equipment such as a bike and sportswear. A Korean karaoke company donates two microphones, and asks Eva to sing a song every week!

Which she does, and no one complains!

PLANNING THE ROUTE

Eva intended to cycle from Shanghai to Istanbul, Turkey, but extends this to cycle from Shanghai to London, UK, adding another 3000 kilometres. WOW!

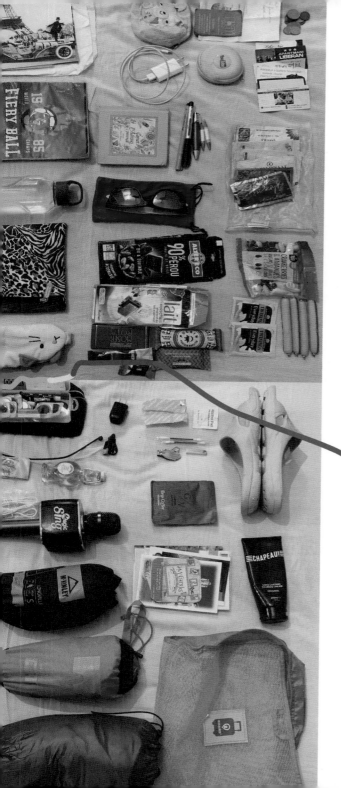

EQUIPMENT

- bicycle, helmet and sunglasses
- double panniers and a backpack
- puncture repair kits
- a tent
- postcards, diary, notebook, a pen and coloured pencils
- various tickets, business cards, souvenirs and gifts
- snacks including bananas and apples in summer, and energy bars and nuts in winter
- change of clothes including tour t-shirt, sleepwear, underwear, socks and shorts
- winter jacket, raincoat and waders
- cyclewear including padded pants, trousers, long sleeve t-shirts, knee socks, sports bra, and fingerless and winter gloves
- toiletries including toothbrush, toothpaste, soap, sun cream, lip balm, shampoo, body lotion, water tissues, eyebrow knife, nail clippers and feminine hygiene
- mobile phone, laptop, chargers, country adaptors, memory stick, microphones and earphones

- needle and thread, disinfectant and plasters
- sleep mask
- butt cream
- passport
- a sense of humour...and chocolate!

PREPARATION PERIOD

Three months before. Eva improves her fitness by joining a cycling club and spinning classes.

INTRODUCTION

WHO IS CHAEWON YOO?

ChaeWon (Eva) is a Korean woman from Seoul, now living in Berlin. She tasted overseas for a short period in the USA as a young child, spent time in Winchester, UK during university, then volunteered for a youth program in Ecuador, South America. After living in Israel as a startup marketing manager, Eva became a business developer in Silicon Valley, California, before working as a tech journalist in Shanghai for three years.

She speaks Korean, English, Spanish, Chinese and German... thirsty for new cultures and situations.

Eva is unconventional and wants to live life to the fullest. Besides cycling, she likes to dance, sing, and paint.

Growing in confidence from a once timid child, Eva is an inspiration to us all!

WHAT IS THE SILK ROAD?

The Silk Road was a network of trade routes connecting East and West, playing a pivotal role in their economic, cultural, political and religious interactions up to the eighteenth century when industrial revolutions saw expansion in domestic productivity, and an era of *enlightenment* and affordability for the masses.

Deriving its name from the lucrative silk trade and protected by the Great Wall of China, many goods and ideas were exchanged, including sciences and technologies such as paper and gunpowder, as well as spreading diseases such as the plague!

WHEN DOES THE TRIP TAKE PLACE?

The trip starts in Shanghai, June 2, 2018, and finishes thirty-six weeks later in London on January 26, 2019. It covers 8,567 kilometres across fourteen countries: China, Kazakhstan, across the Caspian Sea by ferry, Azerbaijan, Georgia, Turkey, Greece, North Macedonia, Albania, Montenegro, Croatia, Italy, Switzerland, France, and the UK, before flying back to South Korea and cycling home from the airport. Eva travels with her Chinese friend, Jianan Lee, up until Turkey.

The following pages are extracts from Eva's diary accompanied by a photographic record and separated into bite-size weekly instalments. Enjoy travelling from East to West with Eva...

WOW!

CYCLING THE SILK ROAD

from Shanghai to London in thirty-six weeks

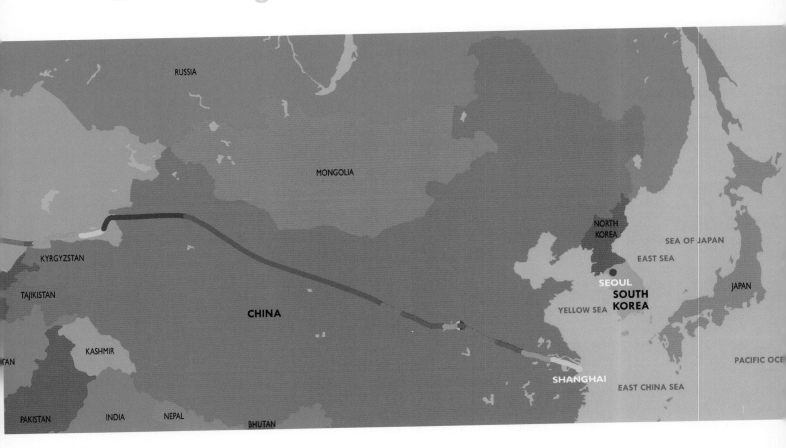

THE START

Turn the page to start travelling East to West chronologically!

Printed in Great Britain
by Amazon

32909241R00048